The Early Furniture of Ontario
and the Atlantic Provinces

The Early Furniture
of Ontario & the
Atlantic Provinces

*A record of the pieces assembled
for the Country Heritage Loan Exhibition
from private collections across Canada.*

Written and selected by Henry and Barbara Dobson

Foreword by Dorothy Duncan
Museums Advisor, Historical and Museums Branch,
Ministry of Colleges and Universities,
Province of Ontario

M. F. Feheley Publishers Co. Limited

Special consultant Rod Brook

Photography – Carl Hyatt

Exhibition sponsored by the Meridian Building Group Ltd.

*To the memory of the
late Mitch Cadeau,
whose gift was rare,
—the perception of quality.*

Foreword

An appreciation of the beauty and worth of the furniture and furnishings of the early homes of Canada came slowly to us all. Within living memory, we have watched those simple yet classic pieces move from the attic and woodshed to a place of honour in our modern and modernized homes. We have inherited a wealth of material to examine, to criticize, to compare, in the form of the once-prized possessions of our ancestors. Our care and concern for its survival is the finest legacy we can leave to further generations.

The furniture of early English Canada, like Canada itself, reflects the influences of the military (who brought their own furnishings with them) and the succeeding waves of immigration and settlement. The French were here first; thus Quebec furniture in the early seventeenth century is a direct copy from the original Louis XIII furnishings brought from the old France to the new. Birch, maple, pine and butternut were used in the construction of these early Canadian furnishings.

After Wolfe, and the ascendency of the English, the influence of the great English cabinetmakers began to assert itself. Possibly the most famous of these was Thomas Chippendale, (1718-1779). His influence is reflected in the many pieces in this book described as 'Chippendale' – chairs with straight grooved legs or ball and claw feet, chests with bracket feet; this was a period of 'masculine' furniture. The fact that many of these pieces loaned came from the Atlantic Provinces is no coincidence, thanks to the large military influence, the proximity to England, and the eastern United States and the fact that furniture was being produced there late in the eighteenth century.

The 'Chippendale' influence asserted itself much longer in Upper Canada because of the great migration from Pennsylvania and New England in the early nineteenth century. Hepplewhite and Sheraton, following after Chippendale, with their lighter, more delicate feminine designs, exemplified a less boisterous age. Their influence came from two directions: direct from England to the finer homes of Canada; and via the United States through the migration to Canada of the United Empire Loyalist families – those colonists who wished to continue to live under the British Crown. The UEL families brought with them their possessions and their knowledge of furniture from the older, more settled former colonies of the United States. Cabinetmaking in the Maritimes reached its greatest flowering in the years between 1780 and 1840, and in Upper Canada after 1800.

The early years of the nineteenth century brought some confusion to Canadian furniture making. The Empire style of furniture from France (named after the Emperor Napoleon), mixed with the Regency styles from England (named after the Prince Regent, later George IV), produced a design intermingling that exhibited touches of both influences. At this time too, the publication of books on cabinetmaking by the Nicholsons, and by George Smith, of England, were studied by, and had a great deal of influence on the furniture makers of Lower and Upper Canada — an influence which continued right up to the end of the nineteenth century.

Throughout the Maritimes and Upper Canada, furniture followed closely the designs of the original homelands of the settlers, with merely local differences from the accepted styles. The great distinguishing mark of Canadian furniture in the whole exists in the use of local woods. Pine, of course, is the best-known and most easily identified, even by the amateur; and there can be few Canadian homes nowadays that do not contain their obligatory piece of highly refinished pine furniture – most often a small occasional item looking slightly lonely among the oiled teak and plastic. There is an often-made assumption among the uninitiated that the early furniture of Canada was made primarily of pine. This is not borne out by the facts.

It was in Ontario and the Maritimes – the furniture which is the subject of this book – that the use of local woods was at its greatest. The more sophisticated, better-trained cabinetmaker worked with bird's-eye and curly maple, both woods were difficult to work with and required more skill than the ordinary joiner. These woods were used for inlays and frames, often with cherry and butternut (stained to look like walnut). Black walnut was often used in chairs and case-pieces; it was easier to work than maple, and tougher and more formal than pine. Cherry, North America's answer to mahogany, was used in tables, chairs, blanket boxes, dressers and cupboards. Pine of course was frequently used more generally by the local joiner than the trained cabinetmaker, to make more utilitarian, less formal pieces. There are, of course, exceptions to the rule. Pine furniture was almost invariably painted, often painted and grained to look like other woods, such as figured maple, mahogany and some-times painted in a joyfully abstract manner. Birch was used for tables, chairs and case-pieces. Some birch wood had an incredible flame pattern which was skillfully fashioned into some very fine pieces.

Each piece is a personal statement by a craftsman whether he learned his craft in England or New England, or in a small town joiner's shop. Unfortunately, here in Canada we have little or no information on cabinetmakers and joiners. We are far behind the United States and England in this matter.

The furniture shown in this book, and assembled and restored so lovingly by its owners, proves that, if nothing else, good design is good design, no matter from which era it comes. How fortunate we are that so much of it is still here with us, not just to be stared at in museums, but serving that purpose for which it was originally made – to be lived with.

Dorothy Duncan,
July, 1974

When we were approached by the Meridian Building Group of Toronto to help them assemble a loan exhibition of furniture, we were at a loss to know in what direction to go. However, after much thought and discussion, we decided that a good starting point would be an exhibition of our own native country furniture, specifically furniture found in the Maritime Provinces and Ontario.

The furniture of the Province of Quebec and the fine furniture of Canada – both English and American – are project contemplations for the future.

The concept of a loan exhibition from private collections is a novel one for Canada, and it is encouraging to see the private sector of business taking this initial step. This exhibition contains country furniture, most of which has never been on public display, and some of which has only been seen by an handful of people. It is the first attempt, and admittedly a pioneer one, to bring together the hand-made furniture of our rural areas for study and analysis, and we hope, for continuing professional or academic activity.

This exhibition will have different meanings for different people; but for the furniture antiquarian, it is significant in that it is probably the first large scale effort undertaken to establish a standard. The criteria was that all pieces must be authentic, with all restorations indicated, and in the case of pine furniture which was either originally decorated or painted, it must either retain the original color or be restored. Show-woods such as walnut, maple, cherry and birch which were intended to be seen need not necessarily retain the original finish. These criteria unfortunately eliminated a great deal of country furniture of superior merit, since in the last 30 years or so, over-zealous dealers and collectors, and yes – even museum curators – with total and complete disregard for the original painted decoration, removed it with misguided vitality that today is appalling to contemplate. This is something of which many of us are guilty.

There were a few exceptions, however, in particular, Mr. and Mrs. Blake McKendry of Elginburg, Ontario and Leslie Donaldson of Galt. The collecting field is richer today because Mr. Donaldson insisted that furniture should be retained in its original finish. As a result of his influence this exhibition is a reality today. The influence of the McKendry's was felt strongly in eastern Ontario. In addition, their arguments were reinforced by the many heated, but friendly discussions which we had with Harris Veitch of Baden, Ontario.

This exhibition is proof that the arguments of these men over the years has had its effect. Original painted finishes on country furniture is now an accepted fact. The interesting thing about 'country furniture' is that it retained the classic influences long after styles had gone out of fashion in the more sophisticated larger centres. In the Maritimes the influences from the American northeastern states and England were felt most strongly, while in Ontario the styles from Pennsylvania continued well into the nineteenth century. Naturally sub-influences occurred in all regions, for example, in Waterloo County in Western Ontario, immigrants from Switzerland and the Alsace created minor diversions.

Unfortunately, we Canadians ignored country furniture during the 1920's and 30's and large quantities were lost to collectors in the United States during that period. Recognition of most Quebec furniture in the U.S. presents no problem, but the pieces from the Maritimes and Ontario have been totally assimilated because of the similarity to American forms.

The furniture in this exhibition is not the furniture of the affluent town or city people. It is the furniture of the common folk – the farmer, the labourer, the tradesman or the fisherman – that level of our culture that has received very little study by the social historian. Country furniture was made by men of varied skills and talents, a lot of it competently made, but of dull design; a small amount of it without restraint of disciplined training but showing imagination and flair. Some of it, such as that found in the Riverjohn area of Nova Scotia, showed sometimes bizarre but never dull aspects. There are many tempting areas for the social historian in Canada to explore this level of society.

We would like to thank the many collectors who have generously loaned their furniture. Their enthusiasm and the assistance they have given has been most encouraging. Not only were the daily routines of their households upset so that these pieces could be photographed, but many have had to live without these pieces for a considerable period of time while they were on loan. In the majority of cases, the furniture shown in this exhibition is in constant daily use by its owners.

There have been some disappointments, of course. Many fine pieces, for example, for a variety of reasons, could not be exhibited, but we do think that in the short preparation time, we have managed to assemble a good cross-section. Not all of the pieces are included for reasons of high design quality, but simply because they are interesting examples of design survival. However, even to the casual viewer, the high quality of the furniture exhibited will be apparent. We see a very encouraging trend today – many young collectors are insisting on inherent qualities such as originality of paint, proportion and form.

Collecting is not merely the acquisition of things. It means preserving a part of our Canadian heritage. There is a very complex range of motives that go into making a collector and they are as dissimilar as the furniture they collect. One of the very strong motivating forces is the sense of delight in discovering and attaining the objects. We sincerely hope this same delight will be shared by the visitors to this exhibition and the readers of this book.

Henry and Barbara Dobson,
July, 1974

Work Tables

1

Delightful folk table from Lunenburg, Nova Scotia with a number of classic influences. Red background with black and yellow trim; a geometric decoration is painted on the top. In original condition. Circa 1850-1860.

CHRISTOPHER, MELISSA AND AUGUSTA BROOK, TORONTO

2

A bird's-eye maple and cherry folk table, from Erbsville, Waterloo County, Ontario. The cherry top is cross-banded with bird's-eye maple, inlaid with four hearts and a six-pointed star in applewood and black ash. The family who owned this table had traditionally believed that it was made by their ancestor, a German immigrant from the Palatinate, as a wedding gift for his daughter. Brasses are original. Circa 1830.

PETER AND SUSAN BELL, SHARBOT LAKE

3

A lamp table in pine and maple, retaining some of the original red color.
This table from Waterloo County, Ontario is of a form seldom seen. No nails were
used in the construction; only pegging and glue-blocking throughout.
Circa 1825.

JOHN AND HEATHER HARBINSON, TORONTO

4

A small barracks-room table of white pine found in Woodstock, Ontario, but probably
part of the furnishings dispersed from the London, Ontario English military post.
The British Ordnance mark, BO combined with an arrow is impressed into one side
of the table. A small door instead of a drawer makes the storage space.
Color: original blue-grey. The primitive construction indicates that it would have been
used by an enlisted man and not an officer. One really cannot date a piece like this
because these military furnishings were made throughout the entire 19th century.

LYNN AND MERLA McMURRAY, TORONTO

5

A small pine side table with scalloped apron and turned legs, from the Mahone Bay area of Nova Scotia. The original paint is black graining over a red base with yellow decorative lining. Circa 1840.

6

A small pine and maple lamp table from the Mahone Bay area of Nova Scotia, grain-painted in red on a deep amber base. This piece is rather heavily proportioned but very attractively decorated. Circa 1840.

LESLIE LANGUILLE, BLOCKHOUSE

7

A small walnut lamp table from the Niagara Peninsula, with a classical line inlay
decoration on drawer front, and a single line inlay on the front face of top.
Circa 1830.

JOHN AND HEATHER HARBINSON, TORONTO

8

A three-drawered cherry Sheraton-style work table. This table is in its original
untouched condition and was found in Waterloo County, Ontario. Molded drawer
fronts are ebonized, a decorative treatment found on many pieces of this period in the
Germanic areas of the Niagara Peninsula and Waterloo County. Circa 1840.

PRIVATE COLLECTION

9

A two-drawered birch and figured maple lamp table with turned legs, found in
Nova Scotia, and retaining the old or original varnish finish. Brasses original.
Circa 1820-1830.

MR. AND MRS. GERALD S. LOWE, AMHERST

10

A pine and maple lamp table found in Wellesley Township, Waterloo County, Ontario. This table is in its original untouched condition. The drawer front bears the stencilled name *Veronika Schultz* and was probably a parental dower gift on the occasion of the daughter's wedding. The Schultzes were an early German family in the Wellesley area. Circa 1840-1850.

PRIVATE COLLECTION

11

A small painted and grained lamp table from Nova Scotia. This country Sheraton-style piece has a thin maple top, attractively shell decorated in brown and ochre. The thin top is a Salem, Massachusetts characteristic. The mahoganized legs are decorated with incised yellow ring turnings. Circa 1830-1840.

ROBERT AND PHYLLIS MEIKLEJOHN, TORONTO

12

A birch lamp table of Sheraton styling from Nova Scotia, with ebonized ring turnings
on legs. Drawer fronts and pilasters have line inlay. Drawer dividers are veneered
in bird's-eye maple. The bottom two drawers are in actuality one deep drawer.
This is an effective method of giving 3-drawer balance to a 2-drawered table.
Condition: original and untouched. Circa 1820-1840.

PRIVATE COLLECTION

13

A pine two-drawered work or lamp table found in the Plattsville, Ontario area.
This table with its dark olive, abstract grained finish, retains the original brasses.
Circa 1850.

PETER AND SUSAN BELL, SHARBOT LAKE

14

A cherry Sheraton-style table found at Brighton, Ontario. This table, with particularly delicate legs, suffered some minor damage in a fire. In refinished condition. Circa 1820.

15

An early 19th century walnut and cherry lamp table. The two drawers are veneered with bird's-eye maple, cross-banded with walnut. Circa 1830.

THE FEHELEY COLLECTION, TORONTO

16

A one-drawered cherry country Sheraton lamp table with notched drop leaves.
Inset veneered panels and drawer front are of bird's-eye maple. Found in Ontario.
Quality of inlay and turnings elevate this table above others of its type.
Circa 1820-1830.

THE FEHELEY COLLECTION, TORONTO

17

A cherry drop leaf table with veneered panel drawer in one end and a dummy
drawer at the other. The inset panelling in the drawer is figured maple with bird's-eye
banding. Secondary wood: white pine. This late Sheraton table belonged to
Archdeacon Nelles, who did pioneer work among the Indians of the Six Nations Reserve
at Brantford, Ontario in the early 19th century. Circa 1825.

JOHN AND HEATHER HARBINSON, TORONTO

Candlestands

18

A very small sawbuck candlestand from the Mahone Bay area of Nova Scotia.
The hand-shaped tapered centre stretcher and chamfered legs form the base for the
solid one-piece pine top. Forged nails throughout. Original red paint. Circa 1800-1830.

LYNN AND MERLA McMURRAY, TORONTO

19

A small tavern table from Gagetown, N.B. This pine table with breadboard ends
has a base coat of red paint, which now has a dark varnish over it.

ROBERT AND JUNE O'NEIL, BOWMANVILLE

20

A small maple rustic candlestand from Mahone Bay, Nova Scotia, in its original paint.
This 18th century stand was made for the house of the present owner. Circa 1770.

E. MACDONALD, MAHONE BAY

21

A late 18th or early 19th century rustic maple candlestand from Nova Scotia
in original red paint, with unusual boot-jack column support.

LYNN AND MERLA McMURRAY, TORONTO

22

A two-tiered pine candlestand found in the Annapolis Valley, Nova Scotia. The original
black-over-red paint is retained. Circa 1830-1840.

GEORGE HOPE, ROSEVILLE

23

A birch candlestand from Nova Scotia, with acanthus-carved support column
and ebonized turnings. In refinished condition. Circa 1820-1830.

GARNET AND PAT TAYLOR, HALIFAX

24

A rustic maple candlestand with old mustard and black original paint. This is a good example of the visual impact of the original paint compensating for an awkward form. Circa 1840.

LESLIE LANGUILLE, BLOCKHOUSE

25

A large painted pine and maple tilt-top table, purchased from the Freeman family,
Amherst, Nova Scotia, who were one of the first settlers in the area. The base is
dark reddish-brown and the top is lighter reddish-brown and cinnamon abstract
graining. Quite often, earlier country furniture forms, such as Queen Anne,
Chippendale, Hepplewhite and Sheraton were decorated at a later period in the
fashionable paints of the early 19th century. Circa 1780-1800.

MR. AND MRS. GERALD S. LOWE, AMHERST

26

A small candlestand from Nova Scotia with octagonal top. Legs are white oak,
column maple, and the top white pine. Circa 1840.

PRIVATE COLLECTION

27

A small Hepplewhite mahogany dish-top candlestand found in the Annapolis Valley,
Nova Scotia. A well proportioned candlestand in its original condition. Circa 1790.

THE LAWS COLLECTION

28

A birch and maple classic-style tilt-top table from Newfoundland. This table retains red wash stain on its centre column. Circa 1790-1800.

BETTY ANN BELL, ST. MARY'S

29

A birch tilt-top candlestand with oval top found in the Liverpool area of Nova Scotia. The original varnish finish is retained. Circa 1800.

JOHN AND VICKI ZINSZER, TORONTO

30

A pine Victorian game table with heavy turned column. The swept legs are given additional support by the segmented pine inserts. The base is painted solid black and the top black with red scroll stencilling and yellow checkerboard. This piece is completely in its 'as found' condition. Circa 1850.

WILLIAM AND LYDIA JOHNSTONE, DETROIT

31

A work table with revolving wool basket made from various hardwoods. It is in its
'as found' condition, retaining the old black paint over red base. This piece is
very similar to Plate 1390 in Wallace Nutting's *Furniture Treasury*.
Found in Lancaster, Ontario. The authors have seen others of this type in the
Woodstock, Ontario area. Middle 19th century.

PRIVATE COLLECTION

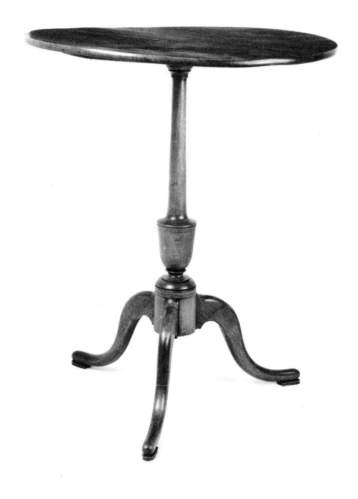

32

A maple candlestand with snake foot, circular top and well-shaped vase on the turned column. In refinished condition. Circa 1800.

GARNET AND PAT TAYLOR, HALIFAX

Dining Tables

33

A small pine sawbuck table in its original untouched condition. This table was found in the Bridgewater, Nova Scotia area. Base and top have the original paint. Table is constructed with forged nails. Circa 1820-1840.

LYNN AND MERLA McMURRAY, TORONTO

34

A sawbuck table with a worn top and retaining a good quantity of the original red paint on the base. This table with breadboard ends has an unusual additional support structure to the sawbuck. Found in the Drumbo area, Blenheim Township, Oxford County, Ontario, it has forged nails in its construction. Circa 1830-1840.

JOHN AND JERI WINE, BRESLAU

35

A pine stretcher-based wall table found in Oxford County, Ontario. Some of the
original red paint is retained: the stretcher is restored. Circa 1820.

PETER AND SUSAN BELL, SHARBOT LAKE

36

A pine and birch stretcher-based table. The longitudinal stretchers are inset from
the legs. This table, with well-worn pine top retains the original blue-green color on
the base. Found in the Mahone Bay area of Nova Scotia. Circa 1830.

LESLIE LANGUILLE, BLOCKHOUSE

37

A stretcher-based table found in the Mahone Bay, Nova Scotia area. The base retains the original or old red. Circa 1780-1800.

LESLIE LANGUILLE, BLOCKHOUSE

38

A pine table with two-board top and maple cabriole legs which terminate in a modified hoof foot. Some of the original red paint is retained. Several tables of this Alsace-Lorraine style have been found in the Waterloo County Area. Circa 1840-1850.

MR. AND MRS. HOWARD PAIN, TORONTO

39

A pine drop-leaf harvest table with the base in old red paint and with a worn dark top.
From the Andrew Lawrie family, Oxford County, Ontario, one of the first Scots
families to settle Blenheim Township. The design of this table is based on a
Scottish style. Circa 1830-1840.

MR. AND MRS. KENNETH KNUCKEY, BADEN

40

A pine drop-leaf stretcher-based harvest table from the Stirling family,
Markham Township, Ontario. The maple base retains the original red paint and the
pine top has been scrubbed. Circa 1825.

PRIVATE COLLECTION

41

A mahogany Chippendale swing-leg table in original condition, found in the
Chandler House, Nova Scotia. Secondary woods: maple and pine. From the style, or
even the secondary wood, one cannot determine whether the table was made
in Canada or the United States. If it is a Canadian table, it was based on an American
design, adopted from an English form. Circa 1770-1790.

ATLANTIC RESTORATIONS LTD., SACKVILLE

42

A maple Hepplewhite-style gate-leg table from the Annapolis Valley, Nova Scotia.
This table has the unusual feature of having three intarsia panels of mahogany
banding in each leaf and the top. Circa 1820.

VERN AND MAGGIE SMART, HAMILTON

43

A mahogany peg-footed Hepplewhite swing-leg table, found in Yarmouth, Nova Scotia. This is a fine country piece with line inlay at each end of the apron and a band of inlay on the peg foot. Secondary woods: birch and white pine. Circa 1800.

PRIVATE COLLECTION

44

The figure in the maple top of this table from the Ottawa area of Ontario is visually emphasized by the spiral treatment of the legs. Circa 1820.

THE FEHELEY COLLECTION, TORONTO

45

A walnut gate-leg table found at Rockton, Ontario. This table is in its original condition. Secondary woods: white pine and cherry. Circa 1825.

JOHN AND HEATHER HARBINSON, TORONTO

46

A cherry Empire-style gate-leg table found in the Niagara Peninsula,
and retaining the original brass castors. Secondary wood: white pine. Circa 1825.

JOHN AND HEATHER HARBINSON, TORONTO

47

A three-part cherry Empire-style banquet table from the St. Thomas, Ontario area.
The legs are acanthus-leaf carved. Circa 1825.

48

This birch sideboard from Amherst, Nova Scotia, has veneered mahogany drawer
fronts, and four brass circles inlaid at each corner of the drawer fronts.
It also has mahogany sock-feet. Circa 1820.

49

A painted five-drawer desk-table or sideboard with arcaded knee-hole found in
Halifax, Nova Scotia. This country Hepplewhite-style desk has legs, drawer dividers,
and top cross-banding in mahoganized paint. The top and drawer fronts are painted
to simulate figured maple. Circa 1820.

ROBERT AND PHYLLIS MEIKLEJOHN, TORONTO

50

A two-drawered pine side table found in Amherst, Nova Scotia, and retaining the red
paint on its base. Circa 1780-1800.

ATLANTIC RESTORATIONS LTD., SACKVILLE

51

A pine folk table with oval top, from Nova Scotia. Forged nails throughout.
The original watermelon pink paint has been retained. Brasses restored.
Circa 1825-1830.

PRIVATE COLLECTION

52

A pine swing-leg tea or card table of American Hepplewhite design. The original
brasses and tortoiseshell decoration are retained. Found in New Brunswick.
Circa 1820.

ROBERT AND PHYLLIS MEIKLEJOHN, TORONTO

Cupboards

53

A small walnut two-part cupboard, found in Hagersville, Ontario, and undoubtedly
made in the Niagara Peninsula. This three-drawered finely made country piece,
with ogee feet and inset quarter columns has drop-leaf table hinges on its doors.
This type of hinge has been found on many pieces of Niagara Peninsula origin.
Ogee feet and brasses restored. Circa 1820.

JOHN AND VICKI ZINSZER, TORONTO

54

A three-drawered cupboard in faded walnut found at Grimsby in the Niagara
Peninsula. This classic-style cupboard with hollow-corner fielded panels
is completely pegged throughout and no nails were used in its construction. Molded
laps to drawer and door edges are ebonized, as are the inset quarter columns
and ogee bracket feet. This outstanding cupboard is in its original untouched
condition, but for three restored drawer pulls. Circa 1825.

CHARLES AND GAY HUMBER, TORONTO

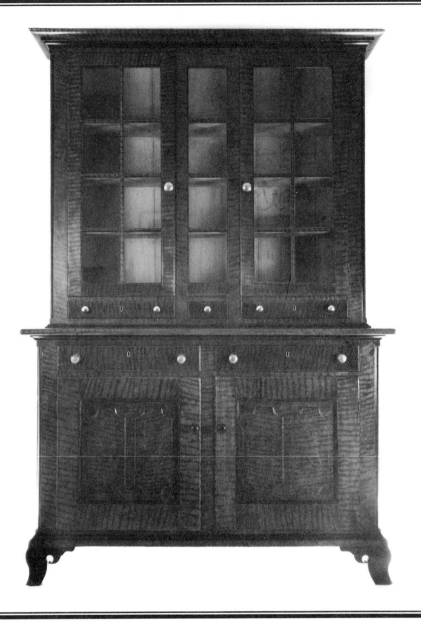

55

A flat-to-the-wall cherrywood Pennsylvania-style cupboard, found in the Niagara Peninsula. An overpaint has been capably lifted to reveal an intact original simulated dark figured maple paint. The well-developed ogee bracket feet are ebonized, as are the inset quarter columns. The two hollow-corner raised panels in the bottom doors are carved from solid pieces of cherry. This is an outstanding cupboard of the 1820-1840 period.

JEANNE TEATHER, FONTHILL

56

A pine cupboard made in East Zorra Township, Oxford County, Ontario, in 1852
by the present owner's great grandfather, Robert Colin Campbell. Campbell
had been a cabinetmaker in Scotland and after emigrating late in life, made
this cupboard using the tools he brought with him. This glazed shoe-foot cupboard
is in a very dark pine finish. Hardware is all original.

CRAIG AND MARGARET McKAY, EMBRO

57

A two-piece black walnut cupboard from the Niagara Peninsula. Fielded panels
on both upper and lower doors, inset quarter columns and ogee bracket feet
are all design features of the fine quality cupboards made in the Peninsula.
Circa 1830-1840.

AUDREY GRIFFITH, JORDAN

58

A Waterloo County, Ontario flat-to-the-wall cupboard, with chamfered corners and
the original red paint. This fielded panel piece typifies the solid-doored cupboards
that were made throughout the Pennsylvania German area of Waterloo County from
the early to middle 19th century. The arched opening above the work surface
was always called a 'pie-shelf.' Circa 1840.

THE LAWS COLLECTION

59

A pine cupboard from Markham Township, Ontario, a Pennsylvania German settlement, north-east of Toronto. The framing of this cupboard is of 2" white pine, and forged nails are used throughout. This outstanding folk cupboard unfortunately had the original paint removed. The owners plan to restore it in the near future. Circa 1820.

JOHN AND HEATHER HARBINSON, TORONTO

60

A large pine corner cupboard, found at Elmira, Waterloo County, Ontario.
This architectural Pennsylvania-style corner cupboard has an outstanding classic,
reeded cornice, herringbone pilasters, fan pendant on the base and four raised
panels on each of the lower doors. A great deal of visual impact is lost by showing
this piece in black and white since it is painted in three colors – blue-green, yellow,
and red. Circa 1825.

JOHN AND VICKI ZINSZER, TORONTO

61

A large pine corner cupboard from Waterloo County, Ontario. Paint and hardware
on this cupboard are completely original, including the interior mustard color.
This basically Hepplewhite-style cupboard has an exterior brown burled
graining paint. Drawer fronts, fluting on frieze and decorative spool turning between
top and base are all mustard colored. Classical architectural features found
in the glazing and the frieze of this rare piece can be seen on houses in various parts
of Waterloo County. Circa 1830.

THE LAWS COLLECTION

62

A small corner cupboard with single door, from the Perth-Waterloo County area
of Ontario. This cupboard of Pennsylvania styling is of a type that was made in great
abundance in Pennsylvania and Ohio, but to a lesser degree in the Germanic
areas of Ontario. It is a good example of decorative paint treatment elevating
a simple form. The quality of the surviving grained mahogany and figured maple paint
is exceptionally good. Circa 1850.

PETER AND SUSAN BELL, SHARBOT LAKE

63

A pine corner cupboard from the Waterloo County area of Ontario. We use the term
'Waterloo County area' to indicate furniture of Pennsylvania and German
styling found in Waterloo and adjoining counties. This early 19th century cupboard
of Pennsylvania styling has its original muted red and amber paint in an excellent
state of preservation. Circa 1830.

ALAN CLAIRMAN, TORONTO

64

A Waterloo County corner cupboard with broken arch pediment. This cupboard,
of Pennsylvania design origin, in a country marriage of Chippendale and Empire styles,
is probably the smallest known example of its type, being only about six feet in height.
Circa 1840-1860.

AUDREY GRIFFITH, JORDAN

65

An open pine architectural corner cupboard from Mahone Bay, Nova Scotia and probably made by one of the late 18th century New England immigrants to Nova Scotia. The original color was a blue-green. Paint and cornice are restored. The majority of this type of cupboard from this area were built-in, as part of the room design. Very few like this one, had backboards of their own, and were therefore portable. Circa 1775-1800.

66

A small three-drawered pine buffet from Waterloo County, Ontario, with an unusual drawer and door arrangement. Some original red color retained. Drawer pulls restored. Circa 1825-1835.

67

From Waterloo County, Ontario, this small pine dish dresser retains some of the
original red paint. Circa 1850-1860.

ELIZABETH HOPE, ROSEVILLE

68

A small white pine open hutch cupboard, found in the Wilno, Ontario area.
This piece retains the original red on the cupboard proper and blue-green on the
cornice. The decorative moldings have been restored. Finely constructed and
pegged throughout, it dates about 1825-1840. Rat-tail hinges restored.

JOHN AND VICKI ZINSZER, TORONTO

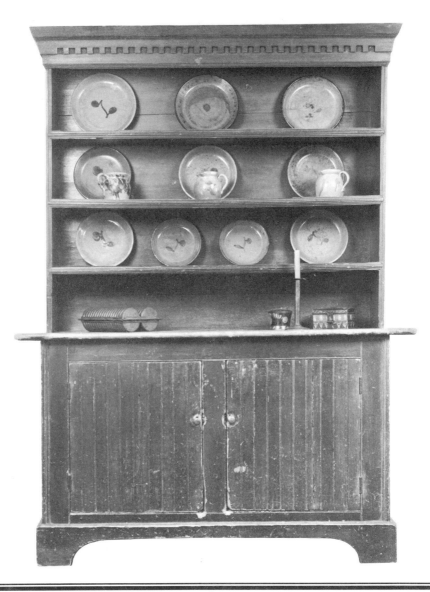

69

A large pine open hutch cupboard from the Rockwood, Ontario area. A great deal
of the visual appeal of this cupboard is due to the severity of line combined
with the original dark forest green paint. The doors are of solid slab construction with
vertical incised lines. Circa 1825-1830.

PETER AND SUSAN BELL, SHARBOT LAKE

70

An open dresser from Newfoundland. The back of this cupboard was formed by the wall against which it originally stood. The back-boards now in it are recent additions to make it portable. The work surface has shaped ends. The remarkable carving on the frieze indicates a Scandinavian influence. Forged nails are used throughout. Remnants of various paints, including the original blue-green and red are evident on the old dark pine. Circa 1775-1800.

ELIZABETH MACDONALD, MAHONE BAY

71

An unusual pine dresser from Glengarry County, Ontario. Possibly made by the
same man who made the one illustrated in *Furniture of Old Ontario* by
Philip Shackleton, Plate 332. This dresser has four open shelves flanked by doors
with two inset molded panels in each. The two paneled doors beneath, have
a molded stile between them. A very interesting decorative feature is the
scalloped molded frieze above the open shelving. Color restored to the
blue-green. Circa 1820-1830.

PRIVATE COLLECTION

72

A very large pewter dresser found north of Toronto, Ontario. It has two fielded-panel
lower doors, flanked by two decorative fielded panels and three drawers above
them. The work surface is 32" deep and over 6' long. The overhanging cornice,
with finely scalloped frieze, lightens and balances the immense size
of this open dresser. Circa 1820.

MR. AND MRS. HOWARD PAIN, TORONTO

Seating

73

A low-back Windsor armchair found in Newfoundland. This rare form has spool and bobbin turnings on legs and H-stretcher base. Its design origin is either English or Scottish. Green color restored. Circa 1760.

LYNN AND MERLA McMURRAY, TORONTO

74

A rustic child's high chair in its original black paint, probably of Ontario origin. Purchased from the Joseph Bower estate, Kitchener, Ontario. Circa 1840.

JOHN AND HEATHER HARBINSON, TORONTO

75

A rustic armchair found in the London, Ontario area. This early 19th century chair is heavily overpainted. Forged nails were used to secure spindles and legs.

LYNN AND MERLA McMURRAY, TORONTO

76

A low-back Windsor armchair, often called a 'firehall chair'. Labelled *W.H. Woodall, Maker, Hagerman's Corners, Markham, C.W.* Original decoration of black over red paint, with yellow striping and gold stencil on back rest. Circa 1860.

PRIVATE COLLECTION

77

A fine late 18th century New England comb-back Windsor armchair with old dark crackled finish and seven-spindled back. Found in Toronto, Ontario.

ALAN CLAIRMAN, TORONTO

78

A very well proportioned rustic comb-back armchair originally owned by the
Reesor family, one of the first Pennsylvania immigrants to settle in Markham
Township, Ontario. Box stretchers would indicate an early to middle 19th century
date. Chair has a black overpaint.

JOHN AND HEATHER HARBINSON, TORONTO

79

One of a pair of rustic armchairs of maple, ash and bass-wood. These chairs,
of decidely English Windsor style, were found on the northern outskirts of Toronto.
Circa 1830.

LYNN AND MERLA McMURRAY, TORONTO

80

A late 18th or early 19th century sack-back Windsor armchair, in dark old,
if not original paint. Found in Nova Scotia.

MR. AND MRS. GERALD S. LOWE, AMHERST

81

A bow-back side chair and a continuous-arm Windsor chair both signed *Humeston*.
Jay Humeston had a chair business in Charleston, South Carolina in 1798
and like many other chairmakers travelled to the Maritime provinces. In 1805,
he advertised Windsor chairs in the Halifax paper, marking them with an iron
brand *J. Humeston, Halifax*. These chairs are in dark, refinished condition
and were originally painted a variety of dark colors.

GARNET AND PAT TAYLOR, HALIFAX

82

A brace-back Windsor side chair with H-stretcher. Found near Liverpool,
Nova Scotia. Some of the original blue-grey paint is retained. Circa 1780.

PRIVATE COLLECTION

83

One of a set of four Sheraton Windsors. These chairs with 9-spindle bow backs were
found in Queen's County, Nova Scotia, and retain some of the original red.
Circa 1800-1820.

THE LAWS COLLECTION

84

An early 19th century Sheraton Windsor armchair with attenuated back support and unusual right-angled arm support. Early finish. Circa 1825.

COLLECTION OF JULIA

85

An early to mid 19th century arrowback armchair, found in Amherst, Nova Scotia. This Sheraton-style chair retains its original reddish-brown crackled finish.

MR. AND MRS. GERALD S. LOWE, AMHERST

86

A 19th century version of an American or English Carver chair reputed to have been found in Newfoundland. It is in 'as found' condition. Circa 1800-1825.

PETER AND SUSAN BELL, SHARBOT LAKE

87

A set of five late Sheraton side chairs with original mahoganized paint with yellow and green decoration. They are branded *Gammon*. Circa 1830.

ELIZABETH MACDONALD, MAHONE BAY

88

A rod-back Windsor rocker found at Preston, Ontario. The original black paint and gilt stencilled decoration are still retained. Circa 1830-1840.

JOHN AND VICKI ZINSZER, TORONTO

89

A side chair from the Burford, Ontario area in its original untouched condition. This chair retains the old brown, crackled varnish finish. Circa 1825-1840.

JOHN AND HEATHER HARBINSON, TORONTO

90

One of three Sheraton arrowback side chairs, found in the Belleville, Ontario area. Originally decorated in three colors. The red base coat survives. Circa 1825-1830.

PRIVATE COLLECTION

91

A small maple high chair with nicely shaped arms and delicate rustic splayed legs in its original dark brown paint. Probably early 19th century. Found in Nova Scotia.

LYNN AND MERLA McMURRAY, TORONTO

92

One of a set of eight side chairs, stamped *Sibley Bros., Lower Stewiacke* in black ink on the underside of the pine plank seats. The Sibley chair is a uniquely Canadian design. Circa 1870.

NICK AND MAGGIE TREANOR, ST. CATHARINES

93

A maple Sibley rocking chair made in Wittenburg, Nova Scotia and shipped from Lower Stewiacke. Original splint seat and stain finish retained. Circa 1860.

NICK AND MAGGIE TREANOR, ST. CATHARINES

94

A set of six chicken-coop side chairs, in original black paint with stencilled decoration. Found in Plattsville, Oxford County, Ontario. Circa 1860-1870.

DAN AND CATHIE STAUFFER, PLATTSVILLE

95

One of a set of five gunstock side chairs, in the original yellow oak graining with dark banding. Circa 1850-1870.

ALAN CLAIRMAN, TORONTO

96

A late writing arm Sheraton rocker in its original paint. Owned by a descendant of
Archdeacon Nelles, who translated the Anglican Book of Common Prayer into the
Mohawk language. Ontario, Circa 1850.

M. NELLES, BRANTFORD

97

A child's maple high chair with original smoke-graining on grey ground, from the
Galt, Ontario area. Circa 1850-1860.

PRIVATE COLLECTION

98

A small rocker from Waterloo County, Ontario, possibly a child's or nursing
rocker. The paint and decoration is restored. Circa 1840-1850.

PETER AND SUSAN BELL, SHARBOT LAKE

99

A maple Queen Anne side chair with Spanish feet, retaining the original red paint. Found in Kentville, Nova Scotia. Probable Connecticut origin. Circa 1725.

THE LAWS COLLECTION

100

A maple Queen Anne side chair from Kentville, Nova Scotia. Probably originated in New England. Old finish. Circa 1725.

THE LAWS COLLECTION

101

A well-designed birch country Chippendale side chair. Found in Liverpool,
Nova Scotia. Circa 1800-1820.

PRIVATE COLLECTION

102

A child's birch high chair from Nova Scotia, retaining original brown paint.
Many designs from remote countries influenced furniture making in the Maritime provinces.
The Chinese style is quite evident here. Early to middle 19th century.

PRIVATE COLLECTION

103

A birch country Hepplewhite side chair. Found in the Annapolis Valley, Nova Scotia, retaining the old finish and the original leather upholstered seat. Circa 1780-1800.

THE LAWS COLLECTION

104

Set of four chairs, one arm and three side, found in New Brunswick.
These birch chairs, with tapered leg and curule shaping in back were reputed to have been made in Saint John. Circa 1820.

ATLANTIC RESTORATIONS LTD, SACKVILLE

105

One of a pair of country Hepplewhite chairs from Amherst, Nova Scotia, with slip seats and H-stretcher. Circa 1800-1820.

PRIVATE COLLECTION

106

A birch country Hepplewhite side chair from the Windsor, Nova Scotia area. The scratch decoration of the back appears to be of a later date. Circa 1790-1800.

PRIVATE COLLECTION

107

One of four small birch side chairs from Newfoundland, of either Scottish or English design origin. Seats and red-brown color restored. Circa 1800.

PRIVATE COLLECTION

108

A maple chair found in the St. Catharines, Ontario area, of country Regency styling. Chair legs have been shortened at some time. Circa 1830.

JOHN AND HEATHER HARBINSON, TORONTO

109

An armchair and a side chair of figured maple from Halifax, Nova Scotia.
In Canada, this style is called 'Regency': in the United States,
it would probably be termed 'Empire'. The chairs are attributed to a Halifax maker
and were doubtless part of a set. Circa 1825.

GARNET AND PAT TAYLOR, HALIFAX

110

A birch country Regency chair with plank seat, found in the London, Ontario area. The old red overpaint apparently was put over original varnish. Circa 1830-1840.

PRIVATE COLLECTION

111

A tapered-leg side chair found in Nova Scotia. This birch chair of country Regency styling is in refinished condition. Circa 1830.

ATLANTIC RESTORATIONS LTD., SACKVILLE

112

One of a pair of maple Regency side chairs, with slip seats. In refinished condition, reputed to have been made in Halifax, Nova Scotia.

LESLIE LANGUILLE, BLOCKHOUSE

113

An Ontario Hepplewhite wing chair. This survival style was made in Leeds County, Ontario. The show wood is mahogany. Circa 1830.

THE FEHELEY COLLECTION, TORONTO

114

A birch country Chippendale wing chair from the Bridgetown, Nova Scotia area. In re-upholstered condition but retaining the original webbing. Circa 1800.

VERN AND MAGGIE SMART, HAMILTON

115

One of a pair of pine rustic corner chairs, found at Madoc, Ontario. These chairs retain a goodly amount of the original red paint. Circa 1850.

PETER AND SUSAN BELL, SHARBOT LAKE

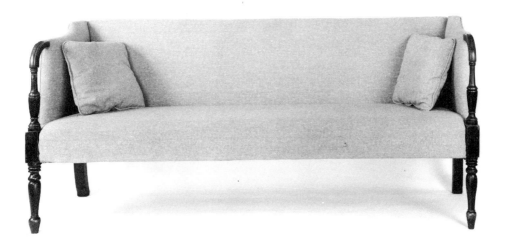

116

A walnut country sofa from Niagara-on-the-Lake, Ontario. This piece,
retains the original untouched finish on the woodwork. Circa 1820-1830.

JOHN AND HEATHER HARBINSON, TORONTO

117

A fine maple Sheraton-style sofa from the Amherst, Nova Scotia area. The show
wood is restored to the original red-brown paint. Circa 1820-1830.

BRETT CAIRNS, KEENE

118

A late 19th century woodbox settle from Waterloo County, Ontario. With its crackled reddish brown paint, this piece is remarkable mainly that such an early Pennsylvania style could have survived so close to the 20th century.

PETER AND SUSAN BELL, SHARBOT LAKE

119

A birch settee with open arms and back with very old, if not original paint
in red, with dark green sailcloth seat cover, a later addition. Found on
the south shore of Nova Scotia, between Lunenburg and Liverpool. Circa 1800.

JOHN AND VICKI ZINSZER, TORONTO

120

An outstanding chair table from the Burford-Simcoe area of southern Ontario.
This table is in its original untouched condition, retaining a rich red-brown
color. The three-board top is splined. Woods: white pine, oak and cherry.
Circa 1800-1820.

JOHN AND VICKI ZINSZER, TORONTO

121

A pine shoe-foot hutch table with hinged seat. This table was found in
Nova Scotia. The color is the original red paint. Circa 1820-1840.

122

A white pine shoe-foot hutch table of small size, in its 'as found' condition, with an old
black paint over the original red. When the top is raised, the hinged seat lifts
to reveal the storage compartment. Found in Nova Scotia. Circa 1800.

LYNN AND MERLA McMURRAY, TORONTO

Desks

123

A pine slant-top desk. This country Hepplewhite piece has dark-grained original paint and an extraordinary depth to the slant lid. Circa 1830.

ATLANTIC RESTORATIONS LTD., SACKVILLE

124

A high painted desk of Hepplewhite styling from the Picton, Ontario district.
This desk retains the original paint, both on the exterior (green) and
interior (green and orange). This piece is very finely modelled with delicate
legs accentuated by edge beading. Hardware original. Circa 1850.

JOHN AND HEATHER HARBINSON, TORONTO

125

A walnut slant-front desk from the Couke family of Embro, Oxford County, Ontario.
Thomas Couke (1815-1890), the original Couke settler at Embro, was the grandson
of George Couke (1757-1812), who was a U.E.L. immigrant who settled in the
Thorold area, near Niagara Falls. The finish and brasses are original. The inner writing
surface conceals a hidden well, which accounts for the false upper drawer.
Late 18th century. Possibly from the U.S.

PRIVATE COLLECTION

126

A mahogany slant-front desk of the middle to late 18th century,
from the Odell family, Halifax, Nova Scotia. This desk, of either English or
Irish orgin has two large carrying handles at its ends, and according to family
tradition had been used as a portable paymaster's desk. Finish is old, if not original.
Brasses original.

MR. AND MRS. KEN KNUCKEY, BADEN

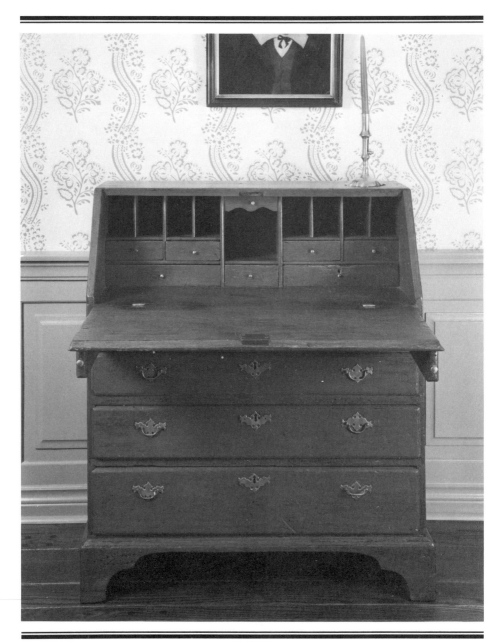

127

A small pine Chippendale slant-front desk with simple interior.
Key hole escutcheons original but drawer pulls restored. This desk retains
exceptional, original red paint. Found in the Saint John
River area of New Brunswick. Circa 1765-1785.

128

A pleasingly proportioned maple Chippendale-style desk from New Brunswick.
Brasses are original. The piece was refinished about 40-50 years ago. The
interior of the desk is well fitted. Circa 1775.

129

A cherry slant, fall-front desk. This piece is attributed to a Mr. Fulton
of Camborough, Ontario in the Niagara Peninsula. The upper case is separate
from the lower and the interior drawer fronts to the writing compartment are bird's-eye
maple veneer. The weakness of the ogee bracket foot indicates a survival style
of the early 19th century. Circa 1840.

JOHN AND HEATHER HARBINSON, TORONTO

130

A fine, figured maple secretary bureau from the Niagara Peninsula.
This Chippendale survival style of the early 19th century is remarkable
for its design restraint. Despite its late period, the form remains unencumbered
by Empire and Victorian influences. One constantly sees this in country
furniture where a particular maker favored a particular style and used it
throughout his whole life. Circa 1825.

THE FEHELEY COLLECTION, TORONTO

131

A Pennsylvania Hepplewhite-style butler's desk, found in Preston, Waterloo County,
Ontario. The exterior of the fall-front of this desk simulates a series of small drawers.
The interior drawers are faced with curled maple. The wooden pulls are not original.
In refinished condition. Circa 1820.

JOHN H. MOORE, LONDON

132

A slant-front applewood desk found at Punkeydoodles' Corners, a cross-roads
hamlet in Wilmot Township, Waterloo County, Ontario. Possibly this desk
was brought by the first Cassel settler from Pennsylvania.
This late Hepplewhite-style desk is in refinished condition with brasses restored.
Circa 1830-1850.

PRIVATE COLLECTION

133

A cherry slant-front desk, found in Waterloo County, Ontario. This desk with a most unusual tapered turned foot, has inset panelled ends with simplified interior. Pulls and escutcheons are original. In refinished condition. Circa 1840.

LOLA HALL, LONDON

134

A crotch-grained mahogany veneered Sheraton writing desk. This simplified, but
fine country desk is of a type that was made throughout the small towns and villages
of New England and the Maritimes. Secondary wood: white pine. In refinished
condition. Circa 1820.

135

An outstanding Empire stand-up desk found in the Kingston, Ontario area
and retaining the original reddish-brown stain. The wood of the case is pine with birch
reeded corner posts and legs. Brasses original. Circa 1830.

PETER AND SUSAN BELL, SHARBOT LAKE

136

A pine slant-front desk from Markham Township, north of Toronto, and signed
Samuel Snider, 1839 . This desk, with dark green paint and sawtooth gallery, is
decorated on the slant lid with a star and other geometric symbols. Drawers are
cross-banded in vermilion and gold; the interior drawers are painted dark green against
a vermilion background. The ends of the desk are abstract-grained.

Mirrors

137

A pine mirror frame, stencilled with the name *Christian Schwarzentruber* and the date *1869* . This was purchased from the family, who were of Swiss origin and living in Baden, Waterloo County, Ontario.

PRIVATE COLLECTION

138

A small early Empire 'tabernacle' mirror in its original condition. This mirror, found in the Amherst area of Nova Scotia has a very naive interpretation of the Egyptian motif on the decorated upper and lower glass panels. Circa 1820.

139

A small 'courting' mirror, in untouched 'as found' condition. This mirror, of probable European origin, was found near Bridgewater, Nova Scotia. Circa 1800.

LYNN AND MERLA McMURRAY, TORONTO

140

A very small Chippendale fretwork mirror found in Sussex, New Brunswick.
This mahogany mirror would be of English, American, or of Maritime
origin. Glass and one broken fret restored. Untouched finish. Circa 1780-1800.

141

A Chippendale country mirror in its original untouched finish, from the Black family
of Amherst, Nova Scotia. The back of the mirror is initialled in ink, *S B* with
the date *1774*.

THE LAWS COLLECTION

142

A Chippendale fretwork mirror with the original glass and old, if not original,
finish. This mirror, found in New Brunswick, could be of either American
or English origin. Circa 1775-1790.

COLLECTION OF JULIA

Storage Boxes

143

A three-drawer blanket box of walnut, from the Niagara Peninsula, with an exceptional Chippendale bracket foot. Circa 1830-1850.

JOHN AND HEATHER HARBINSON, TORONTO

144

A birch sugar chest from Wolfville, Nova Scotia, referred to by the family who owned it
as the 'Planter's chest'. People from Virginia, called 'Planters', formed a
separate immigration wave from colonial America to Nova Scotia.
This 18th century chest had turned legs applied in the early 19th century.
Modifications of this sort were frequently done later. Although the basic box, for
storing cone sugar, shows earlier influences, styles in country furniture were perpetuated
long after they had gone out of fashion in urban areas. The original oval marine
brasses, with shell, spear and trident motifs, date the box in the 1775-1780 period.

145

A four-drawered lift-top Empire blanket box, with mahoganized grained finish.
Found in the Kingston, Ontario area. The applied split balusters are painted a dark green.
Circa 1830.

LYNN AND MERLA McMURRAY, TORONTO

146

A pine lift-top blanket box with a false upper drawer, found in the Belleville area of Ontario. The ends are recessed with molded panelling. An old red overpaint covers the original grey. Brasses restored. Circa 1840.

PETER AND SUSAN BELL, SHARBOT LAKE

147

A decorated immigrant chest found at Milverton, Perth County, Ontario.
This chest is from either the French or German Palatinate.

LYNN AND MERLA McMURRAY, TORONTO

148

A large sponge-decorated blanket box, in mustard color. Wood: pine.
Purchased from the Freeman family, Amherst, Nova Scotia. See also number 25.

MR. AND MRS GERALD S. LOWE, AMHERST

149

A pine blanket box from Wellesley, Waterloo County, Ontario. Original black graining over red. Inscribed *Alan Ament, John Ament, Wellesley, C.W., 1854.*

CHARLES AND GAY HUMBER, TORONTO

150

A pine blanket box found in Lunenburg County, Nova Scotia, with an exceptional sponge-painted decoration. Circa 1820-1830.

LESLIE LANGUILLE, BLOCKHOUSE

151

A white pine painted box. Molded strapping is painted the original green. The inset panels on the top and front are the original red. Circa 1820-1830.

ATLANTIC RESTORATIONS LTD., SACKVILLE

152

A large seaman's chest found in Nova Scotia and bearing the name *G.M. Neves* on its faded green painted surface. All paint is original. Early 19th century.

IAN AND CAROL ANDREWS, DIGBY

153

A painted dome-topped box from the Niagara Peninsula; the original paint in yellow, green, orange and brown. Circa 1820-1830.

PETER AND SUSAN BELL, SHARBOT LAKE

154

A small document box purchased from the Joseph Bower estate.
The base color is charcoal grey, and houses and random strokes are dark red with dirty white dots throughout. All original paint. Early 19th century.

PRIVATE COLLECTION

155

A small dome-top painted box from the Niagara Peninsula. Colors are yellow, cinnamon and deep red-brown. Circa 1820.

JOHN AND HEATHER HARBINSON, TORONTO

156

A small 18th century mahogany strongbox found in the Goderich, Ontario area. Decorated with a scene and the painted letters *Banks o' Clyde Friendly Society.*

PRIVATE COLLECTION

Dressers

157

A walnut Chippendale high chest of drawers, from the Niagara Peninsula.
This chest has finely reeded inset quarter columns and frieze, and unusual attenuated
ogee bracket feet. Brass are original and of the early 19th century,
thus dating the chest about 1825.

JOHN AND HEATHER HARBINSON, TORONTO

158

A walnut Niagara Peninsula chest of drawers in the 19th century Chippendale survival
style. This piece is in its original untouched condition, also retaining the
original glass pulls. It has ebonized quarter columns and boldly shaped molding
under the top, shaped back-board and an interesting ebonized spindle gallery.
Circa 1840.

AUDREY GRIFFITH, JORDAN

159

A cherry survival Chippendale-style chest of drawers from Jordan, Niagara Peninsula.
This chest retains the original finish and glass pulls. There is a chalked date
of 1837 on the underside of the bottom drawer. Ebonized inset quarter columns and cove
molding on top and bottom of the case provide decorative treatment.

JOHN AND HEATHER HARBINSON, TORONTO

160

A walnut chest of drawers with plain inset walnut quarter columns and molded drawer
edges. Chests of drawers of this type have been found in the Niagara Peninsula
in such quantity, that there can be no doubt as to their origin.
This chest reputedly belonged to a Sherk family in Waterloo County, Ontario.
There have been many pieces found in Waterloo County which were owned by families
who were part of a secondary migration from the Niagara Peninsula.
Circa 1830-1840.

JOHN AND HEATHER HARBINSON, TORONTO

161

A solid bird's-eye maple Ontario chest of drawers. Brasses are restored.
This chest has excellent proportions and a fully developed robust Chippendale ogee
bracket foot. The plain inset quarter columns and half-round molded edges
on the top indicate a date of about 1830.

JOHN AND HEATHER HARBINSON, TORONTO

162

A cherry Hepplewhite high chest of drawers with original brasses and old if not original crackled finish. This piece was brought into the Mahone Bay, Lunenburg County area from Pennsylvania. Secondary wood: tulipwood. Circa 1780-1790.

PRIVATE COLLECTION

163

A well proportioned butternut and birch Hepplewhite chest of drawers,
found in the Brockville, Ontario area. The feet have an excellent splay. Brasses restored.
Circa 1830.

JOHN AND HEATHER HARBINSON, TORONTO

164

A bow-front chest of drawers from Amherst, Nova Scotia. There have been several
pieces of furniture of similar construction and inlay seen in this area,
all obviously by one maker. Drawer fronts are bird's-eye maple veneer with ebonized
line inlay. Secondary woods: birch and white pine. Circa 1825-1830.

JOHN AND VICKI ZINSZER, TORONTO

165

A strikingly figured birch chest of drawers of Sheraton styling from Nova Scotia,
in refinished condition. Brasses restored. Many of these early chests underwent several
changes in drawer pulls. This one had at least two sets prior to those
seen here. Circa 1820.

PRIVATE COLLECTION

166

A cherry chest-on-chest from Waterloo County and originally from the Steckley family.
This piece has similar inlay to number 175 and the shell pendant, although cruder,
is similar to that of number 167. The drawer dividers are veneered
in cherry and the faces of the small upper drawers in bird's-eye maple.
Drawer pulls are replacements. This piece is one of an interesting group of early
classic-style pieces found in Waterloo County, Ontario. Circa 1820.

JOHN AND JERI WINE, BRESLAU

167

A cherrywood chest of drawers found in Waterloo County, Ontario. Brasses restored.
This American-style chest of classic design, features a sand-burnt inlaid shell
on the base pediment, and line and dot inlay above the undulating skirt.
This type of inlay is a decorative characteristic of Baltimore furniture. It will be seen that
the case and the skirt are very similar to number 168. Circa 1815-1820.

168

A cherrywood chest of drawers in the classic style, featuring a simple horizontal band
of maple inlay above the shaped skirt. Brasses restored. Found in
Waterloo County, Ontario. Circa 1825.

JOHN AND VICKI ZINSZER, TORONTO

169

A high chest of drawers from the Niagara Peninsula, Ontario, with an outstanding painted and grained finish, simulating figured maple and mahogany. The classic-style gallery is ebonized. Drawer pulls are original: feet are restored. Circa 1850.

JOHN AND HEATHER HARBINSON, TORONTO

170

A pine Empire chest of drawers from Waterloo County, Ontario, with a striking
painted finish in reddish-brown and cinnamon, to resemble crotch-grained mahogany.
Half-round ebonized pilasters are stencil-decorated. Circa 1840.

171

A small pine chest of drawers from Newfoundland. This chest of country Empire styling,
retains some of the original red paint. Porcelain knobs are probably original.
The decorative treatment on the drawer fronts that appears to be line inlay, was done
by a hand tool which compressed the surface of the wood. Circa 1850.

PRIVATE COLLECTION

172

A pine folk wardrobe from Pictou County, Nova Scotia, which was originally painted blue.
Although not folk furniture in the true sense, as a folklorist understands it,
the term indicates to the public a style, a type of carving, a kind of painting, etc.
The people who made these things had no knowledge of pattern books,
but simply were basing their creations on things they had perhaps seen in their locality.
The whimsical structure on top apparently was made to hold hats.
Forged nails were used throughout. Circa 1800-1830.

ALFRED SAULNIER, HALIFAX

173

A pine and maple one-piece wardrobe, from the Roman Catholic village of Maryhill,
which up until World War II was called New Germany. The front door of the house
from which this piece was removed is carved in identical motifs.
The Franco-German style is clearly seen in the carved panels of the door and the
rounded cornice. It is quite interesting to see a piece of this late date with rat-tail hinges.
Some of the original red color remains. Circa 1840-1850.

PRIVATE COLLECTION

174

A pine wardrobe with rat-tail hinges, from Lisbon, a little hamlet in Perth County,
Ontario. It is decorated in plum colored paint with lighter suggestions of gothic
arches in the rectangular panels. Another piece from one of the Alsatian settlements
of the Waterloo County area. Circa 1830-1840.

175

A cherry wardrobe, with maple and walnut inlay, found in Baden, Waterloo, Ontario.
Earlier Pennsylvania wardrobes of this type were of heavier and coarser design.
This early 19th century piece shows a remarkable degree of refinement
due to the influence of the American Federal period. Any further refinement would result
in a weakened design. Door brasses original; those on the drawers are restored.
Circa 1825.
Two other cherry wardrobes of very similar style, but lesser design quality, and
obviously made by the same craftsman are known. All were found in Waterloo County.

HENRY AND BARBARA DOBSON, PLATTSVILLE

176

A walnut linen press from the Niagara Peninsula, with a very plain concave cornice, four inset panels in the doors and the usual arrangement of two drawers over one long one in the bottom storage area. The base is a simple bracket with slightly flared feet.
Written on the back in old script are the initials *J.G.* with the date *1830*.
This is an excellent example of a simple, crisp country-styled piece of furniture.

ALAN EMERSON, ORILLIA

177

A walnut Pennsylvania-style linen press, originating in the Niagara Peninsula. This well proportioned cupboard has the lower three drawers edge-banded in figured maple. The two upper doors have decorative applied molding. Finely modelled ogee feet, inset reeded quarter columns, reeded frieze and impeccable construction create a superior country case piece. Circa 1820.

THE FEHELEY COLLECTION, TORONTO

178

A two-piece walnut linen press, found in the Niagara Peninsula.
This linen cupboard of American late 18th century classic design is of impeccable
country craftsmanship, with the entire back being pegged. Although the proportioning
of this cupboard is slightly awkward, it still has very high quality
of design and workmanship. Circa 1820-1840.

JOHN AND HEATHER HARBINSON, TORONTO

Beds

179

A pine cradle from Waterloo County, Ontario, with the original brown grained paint. Made in the early 19th century.

JOHN AND HEATHER HARBINSON, TORONTO

180

A hooded cradle from Nova Scotia with excellent scrolling on hood but rather crude rockers. Original red paint. Circa 1820.

CAROL AND IAN ANDREWS, DIGBY

181

A rustic pine cradle from Petite Rivière, Nova Scotia, in 'as found' condition.
This cradle was made with forged nails and has late 18th or early 19th century repairs.

HARRY AND TILLIE PORTER, MARTIN'S RIVER

182

A child's single bed of Empire styling from Waterloo County, Ontario, held
together by wooden pegs and retaining the original red paint. Circa 1840.

THE LAWS COLLECTION

183

A maple trundle bed with pine head and foot boards, retaining some of the original red. This bed has the original wooden wheels which permit it to be rolled out from under the side of a large bed. Found in Waterloo County, Ontario. Circa 1830-1840.

184

A small pine and maple child's bed in the original red paint, found in the
Niagara Peninsula. This Empire-style bed could be considered representative of the
1830-1850 period.

JOHN AND HEATHER HARBINSON, TORONTO

185

A maple 'cannonball' bed found in Woodstock, Ontario. Exhibiting Sheraton influence in the lower turnings of the legs and the spindles of the headboard. Circa 1850.

186

A good example of an early 19th century Queen Anne-style bed made entirely of pine, with the original dark brown paint. Found in Markham Township, Ontario.

187

A walnut Empire-style canopy bed from the Niagara Peninsula. This bed does not display the coarseness or heaviness of most country beds of the Empire style.
Circa 1830-1840.

JOHN AND HEATHER HARBINSON, TORONTO

188

A Sheraton tester bed with the original red finish and canopy frame. The head posts
on these early beds were usually simply turned because they would be hidden
by the hangings. Although found in the Maritimes, this bed is of New England origin.
Circa 1850.

LYNN AND MERLA McMURRAY, TORONTO

189

A maple bed from Mahone Bay, Nova Scotia. The foot posts have a squared foot
to the waist with turned upper section. Head posts are square tapered throughout.
Restorations to foot and head boards. Posts retain the original red paint.
This bed was made for the house of its present owner, which was built in 1770.
See also number 20.

E. MACDONALD, MAHONE BAY

190

A small birch pencil-post canopy bed with shaped pine head and foot boards.
This bed was found in the village of Lancaster in eastern Ontario. Tester replaced.
Circa 1790-1800.

Miscellaneous

191

A dressing table from the Alsatian settlement in Waterloo County, Ontario.
This white pine table is based on a French Louis XVI style *poudreuse*. The cherrywood
tambour is backed with canvas. Upper gallery, red paint and brasses restored.
Circa 1830-1840.

PRIVATE COLLECTION

192

A small pine washstand found in the Liverpool area of Nova Scotia
with stencilled splash-board and drawer front of red and black, and abstract
painting on the top and shelf. Circa 1850.

MR. AND MRS. HOWARD PAIN, TORONTO

193

A Nova Scotia pine folk Victorian washstand, restored to the original red color.
Circa 1850.

HARRY AND TILLIE PORTER, MARTIN'S RIVER

194

A rare small bow-front dry sink of maple and pine, retaining the original red paint finish.
This piece was found in an area of Waterloo County, Ontario, settled by people
from Alsace-Lorraine. Circa 1830-1840.

JOHN AND HEATHER HARBINSON, TORONTO

195

A mid-19th century dry sink of Chippendale survival style found in Perth County, Ontario. This is a well constructed piece with dove-tailing to the case and bracket feet. The wine-red color has been restored. Circa 1840-1850.

MARIANNE SCOTT, AYTON

196

A large dry sink with canted well, above double doors, which have fielded panels.
This piece was found in the St. Catharines area of the Niagara Peninsula.
Although the sink was originally painted green, removal of an overpaint left only
vestiges of that color on the old dark pine. Circa 1850.

PRIVATE COLLECTION

197

A fish-tail hanging corner cupboard of white pine from Wellesley, Waterloo County, Ontario. Blue-green color restored. Circa 1840-1850.

PRIVATE COLLECTION

198

An 18th Century tall-case clock with arched hood, in cherry and pine.
Panels are fielded in the arched door. The case extends below the simple base
molding to form the feet. Family tradition says that this clock was brought from
Warren County, New Jersey by a member of the family, one Conrad Book, in 1797,
to the Niagara Peninsula where it was found.

NICK AND MAGGIE TREANOR, ST. CATHARINES

199

A tall-case clock found in Dundas, Ontario. Marked *S. Thomas, Plymouth*.
Inscribed on the door *PRO REGIAT GREGE*. Circa 1820.

CHARLES AND GAY HUMBER, TORONTO

200

This rustic pine clock, found north of Toronto, is identical to those made by
Silas Headley, a Connecticut clockmaker. Original dark paint. Circa 1825.

PRIVATE COLLECTION

201

A small pine footstool reputed to have come from the Saint John River Valley
of New Brunswick. This stool, with richly carved top, is painted old mauve, blue, red
and yellow, and this paint is in an excellent state of preservation. Circa 1850.

ROBERT AND JUNE O'NEIL, BOWMANVILLE

202

A small pine footstool from the Amherst, Nova Scotia area. Top is well worn
with an excellent patina. Base is decorated in black and yellow on a dark green ground.
Circa 1840.

LYNN AND MERLA McMURRAY, TORONTO

203

A pine Niagara Peninsula footstool, found in the Grimsby, Ontario area.
It still retains the original red paint, but has been reupholstered. Middle to late
19th century.

PRIVATE COLLECTION

204

A Victorian miniature slant-front bureau. It retains the original untouched crackled mustard-colored paint. Brasses original. Circa 1850-1860.

MR. AND MRS. GEORGE MURRAY, CAMBRIDGE

205

A small rustic lap desk from the Black family, Amherst, Nova Scotia. Brass hinges are original. Color is original red. Circa 1800.

MR. AND MRS. GERALD S. LOWE, AMHERST

206

A small pine 'prim' or document box, purchased from the Black family of Amherst,
Nova Scotia. It retains the old red paint. Early 19th century.

MR. AND MRS. GERALD S. LOWE, AMHERST

207

A small trinket box from the Lunenburg area of Nova Scotia, with applied carvings
and a slide lid. The original color is retained – yellow with carvings in red.

MRS. WALTER ANNIS, LUNENBURG

208

A pine mantel found at St. Catharines, Ontario. This classic-style mantel could have
been made in the Niagara Peninsula, but more likely was carved and brought
to the Peninsula from Pennsylvania. Color restored to the approximate original wine.
Circa 1790-1810.

THE LAWS COLLECTION

209

King William III painted on a table top from the Orangeville, Ontario area. Obviously from a local Orange Hall. Probably copied from an old Currier lithograph such as the one below. Brown background with red and blue decorated border. 3' x 4½'. Circa 1860.

ROD BROOK, TORONTO

ADDENDA

Our most special thanks in this area go to Mr. Louis Bodnar of Kitchener, Ontario for lending a large part of his textile collection which colorfully complements the furniture.
The following have lent other furnishings which, while not photographed, play an important part in this exhibition.

PETER AND SUSAN BELL, SHARBOT LAKE
Waterloo County christening spoon
Waterloo County showtowel

ROBERT AND PHYLLIS MEIKLEJOHN, TORONTO
Portrait of two sisters by Ida C. Jones
Portrait of a Nova Scotia ship

HARRY AND TILLIE PORTER, MARTIN'S RIVER
Portrait of the barque 'Amanda', built on the Noel shore of Nova Scotia
    for O'Brien interests, 1885

ELIZABETH MacDONALD, MAHONE BAY
Spinning wheel from Mahone Bay, N.S.
Quilt on canopy bed

MR. AND MRS. GERALD S. LOWE, AMHERST
Nova Scotia quilts and samplers
Mammy's bench in original paint

LESLIE LANGUILLE, BLOCKHOUSE
Circular carving from box
Drum

THE LAWS COLLECTION
Komoka woven coverlet

MR. AND MRS. GEORGE MURRAY, GALT
Labelled wool winder

LYNN AND MERLA McMURRAY, TORONTO
Ship portrait
Horse carving

COLLECTION OF JULIA
Small box from N.S.

GARNET AND PAT TAYLOR
Spinning wheel
Painting – watercolor of Lunenburg, N.S. by Comingo. Early 19th century

RON AND ROSE O'HARA, ST. MARY'S
Collection of stick spatter dishes

W.M. THOM, KITCHENER
Print of the Battle of Queenston, dated 1813

JOANNE CADEAU, SAINT JOHN
Painted blanket box from Perth County, Ontario
Dome-topped box found in Ontario

SHIRLEY AND MURRAY EDWARDS, WOLFVILLE
Set of 6 bird-cage Windsor side chairs with seven-spindle backs, in original
    brown paint, found in Mahone Bay, N.S.

ALAN EMERSON, ORILLIA
Panelled cupboard from Puslinch Township, Ontario, restored paint
Glazed-door cupboard
2-drawer blanket box

CHARLES AND GAY HUMBER, TORONTO
Black homespun coverlet with flower and thistle embroidery

ALAN CLAIRMAN, TORONTO
Pair of painted chairs with maple graining

This book was designed by Hugh Michaelson
Typeset in 10 point Garamond by The Moore Type Foundry Ltd.
with printing film supplied by Campbell Peterson Graphics Limited
and printed on 80 lb. Wellington Offset by The Alger Press Limited.